By Christopher Dow

Fiction
Effigy
    Book I: Stroud
    Book II: Oakdale
The Books of Bob
    Devil of a Time
    Jumping Jehovah
The Clay Guthrie Mysteries
    The Dead Detective
    Landscape with Beast
    The Texas Troll Unlimited
    Darkness Insatiable
Roadkill
The Werewolf and Tide, and Other Compulsions

Nonfiction
Lord of the Loincloth (nonfiction novel)
Book of Curiosities: Adventures in the Paranormal
Occasional Pilgrimage: Essays on Film, Literature, and Other Matters
Living the Story: The Meandering, True, and Sometimes Strange
        Adventures of an Unknown Writer
    Vol.I: Growing Up Takes a Long Time
    Vol. II: Growing Old Takes Longer

Martial Arts
The Wellspring: An Inquiry into the Nature of Chi
Circling the Square: Observations on the Dynamics of Tai Chi Chuan
Elements of Power: Essays on the Art and Practice of Tai Chi Chuan
Alchemy of Breath: An Introduction to Chi Kung
Leaves on the Wind: A Survey of Martial Arts Literature (Vol. I–VI)

Poetry
City of Dreams
The Trip Out
Texas White Line Fever
Networks
A Dilapidation of Machinery
Puzzle Pieces: Selected Poems

Editor
The Abby Stone: The Poetry of Bartholo Dias
The Best of Phosphene
The Best of Dialog

A Dilapidation of Machinery

A Dilapidation of Machinery

Christopher Dow

Phosphene Publishing Company
Temple, Texas

A Dilapidation of Machinery

© 2022 by Christopher Dow
ISBN 13: 978-1-7369307-2-4

Published by:
Phosphene Publishing Company
Temple, Texas, USA
phosphenepublishing.com

1.5

For Julie

Contents

A Dilapidation of Machinery

Collective Sentiments

I Need Something to Work

I need something to work.
Maybe this will work.
It must work, has to work.
If it doesn't work....

Needless to say, it didn't work
Though I tried to make it work.
I've tried often to make it work,
But it never seems to work.

Calmly explaining the facts
Doesn't always work, either.

Circumstance of Denial

When it comes to false accusations,
The best lies are always those
Where denial lies thick as increase
And circumstance is circular.

When we act wrongly—
Not with malice, perhaps,
But often with great stubbornness—
We stab our own hearts,
For there is particular pain
In mastering denial that cannot
Be a distraction du jour.

All systems are more complex than we can know—
Equations of strange code with no solutions,
Only a trembling, prolonged string of cyphers
In perfect denial of cool pain.

'Round and 'Round

'Round and 'round we go, child,
On the Ferris Wheel:
'Round and 'round the engineer's
Ferrous wheel.
'Round and 'round the lover's
Fair ass wheel.
'Round and 'round behind the getaway driver's
Fear as wheel.
'Round and 'round, she shouldn't wear that with her
Flair ass wheel.
'Round and 'round go those fancy hubcaps when
Flair is wheel.
'Round and 'round, and so goes fashion when
Flair is real.
'Round and 'round goes the paranoid whose
Fear is real.
'Round and 'round we go.
'Round and 'round.

It's Not What Happens

It's not what happens that's important.
It's who you are and how and why
You do what you do.
The most irksome:
The vapid, crude, and acquisitive,
Doing what they do to damage
And take advantage of others
For the most mundane and self-serving of reasons.
Or just out of love of cruelty.

Life in this reality is just so limited.
I long for horizons broader
Than a squabble over the name of God
Or some minor difference
In the manifestation of one's humanity.
I look for a shore where ignorance and fear
Do not harbor with greed and violence,
Where selfishness exists in making life
A better place for everyone
Because you are one of those everyones.
Instead we face the kind of selfishness
That enslaves and exploits others
So that the perpetrators
Can falsely stand above
While manifestos die in a flood
Of a chaos in which too many
Have lost sight of up or down.
So give me your how and why
Instead of who and do,
And if you don't,
I can only assume the worst.

To the IHOP Hostess

Hostess: A woman who welcomes
guests to a public dining room.

The restaurant, nearly empty
This early, drizzly Sunday morning.
Three large rooms
Arranged one behind the other,
Only two or three tables occupied,
All in the front room.
More staff than guests.
You, young, immature in the ways of a world
Larger than you imagine or understand,
Stiffened instantly when we entered,
Almost jumped out of your skin
To shout your outrage from tight lips
Beneath eyes blazing at our affront
To your sense of decency and racial propriety:
Me white, my wife black.
On holy Sunday, for Christ's sake!
Church time in the Old South.

You said nothing, just snatched two menus
From their holder,
Showed us your stiff back,
Led us out of sight
Of the tables at the front,
Through the completely empty second room,
To outcast us into the also empty third room,
Up against back windows
Looking out not over the green museum grounds

Across the grayly glistening street in front,
Trees heavy with mists,
But over the back alley.
Where we could not be seen.
Where we were out of your sight.
You threw the menus
Onto the table without a word,
Turned away, stomped off,
Back rigid, head rigid on rigid neck,
And we did not see you again,
Even when a few other diners came in
To be seated in the front room by a waitress.
Obviously you were very disturbed.

It's happened to us before,
Where we've been seated in isolation
In other back rooms, on back patios.
But the irony, dear IHOP hostess,
Is that you could not have seated us better:
Away from your righteous anger,
Overlooking an alley
Whose stuccoed brick wall,
Stained, cracked, flaking
Was a marvelous study in pattern, texture, and form
To rival any of the art
In the museum across the street.

The waitress arrived,
More mature than you, dear hostess,
Amusement gleaming in her eyes
At your overwrought outrage.
She had no fear of us, no hatred.
She's a waitress, by god.
She's seen it all.

When we left, Julie took a photo of the wall
To turn its intricate imagery into art.
Isn't it amusing, dear hostess,
That a stained and flaking back alley brick wall
Is so much more interesting and inviting than you?

Auto Daffy

On the way to work,
My carb intake was too great,
Leaving me revved up
Until I braked, tired and exhausted.
Afterward, my boss grilled me
Then gave me the boot,
And as I left the parking garage,
Some hood stuck me up,
Committed asphalt and battery,
Leaving me racked and stacked.
Though I was getting mixed signals,
I sped home, petal to medal,
And as I wheeled into the driveway,
I found a bumper crop waiting
For a lube job.

A Few Questions About Zombies

Do zombies ever get full?
If so, do they stop being hungry
And just want to relax on the sofa
And watch TV or read a good book
While they digest their meal?
Can they die of starvation?
Do they have to piss and take a shit
After eating all that raw, raw meat?
Do they prefer tender babies
To tougher adults?
Do they get horny
Or bored with their limited zombie non-lives?
And if muscles and tendons naturally decay,
And are eaten up by bugs and other critters,
Why don't their dead bodies rot and fall apart?
How do they stay in one piece
Much less move faster than you can escape?

What I Say to Mean

1

The concept of relevance,
Most necessary, is most rejected
In ceremonies of hampering,
In malignant purpose,
By rituals that govern all things.
Mere fidelity to rule,
Even free of contamination,
Eventually misleads to distortion:
The realm of being objective
Is a refuge free of personality
Or of absolute immersion in it.

2

Comparison would have allowed me to discover more,
Would have forbade any manifestation
That remained in the way of avoiding ghosts.
But I was denounced by other events
And reintroduced to strange distortions
Until all I had left was a masterpiece of mythic allusions
And transcendental scenarios that range
From omnipotence to abject passivity,
From compassion to mean-spiritedness.

Critically examined transcendental scenarios
Evolve from administered morality—
Without the distortion and error of illusion,
Without the agitation of an itinerant response
Heretical with materialistic assets

That the Gods themselves have produced.
The personal and transcendental await
In selfless and spontaneous power.
In boundless and sublime perfection.

Instead, what we see, we quickly bury
In the flesh of skeletal gardens
Where plants sere,
Shriveled out of shape,
Twisted out of true,
Join the scenario for greater effect.

Form, when normal and accepted,
Has much in common with this myth
Of imaginary earthly figures
That conceals the cosmology of history
Within the phenomenon of a dead
And miraculously suspended body.

3

Relationships between people are as brief as they are various,
And the power you give to others is really your own.
Along with the destruction of the origin myth of the usual,
A period of revitalization operating on culture as a whole
Assumes the role of guide and embodies
A new storytelling with the old order of etiquette.

Concepts abound when polytheism
Is not a term separating poverty from riches
But is constituted of the memory
Of subtle investigations that transmit the doctrine,
Pure and integral, without any attenuation,
As though movement caused it
To shed its skin to reveal the true serpent
Of the flow of time.

Seesaw Trajectory

Youghiogheny River

I dare you to pronounce the name.
Locals just call it the Yuk.
The lower channel dusky teal
Shading almost to turquoise
As it climbs and shallows
Alongside the rail line,
Ever rockier and abundant outcrops,
Creating rapids.
Seeking headwaters
To move past them.

Along its banks, far from anything,
Cabins sit, bucolic, remote.
Who are these people
Living the life of a century past?

Often we must deviate
As both we and the river
Keep moving without pause,
Along our own paths,
In our own times.

The headwaters fracture
Into gullies and creeks
That vanish into the past
As the train burrows
Through the heart of a mountain—
Pitch black nightmare darkness,
Sudden and profound.
Waiting for the next light.

Married to a Lifestyle

You must have this—
Pure desire to be more
Than you are projected
Upon store window glass.
The image you hunger for
But cannot possess
Because it is but an image
Upon the glass, no more real
Than a ghost until,
In your desire to possess
And achieve fruition,
You succumb, and with a flash
Of cash, you make the window barrier
Vanish.

Yet you are still you,
And there...Over there!
It's another store window!

The Engineer's Memory of Clouds

Tattered and torn
Battered and worn.
You gotta think more than twice
About crossing a love like that:
Beautiful,
Caring,
Mysterious,
Nurturing,
Smart.

We each do what we do,
And that's what happens,
But when you take ownership of something,
It takes ownership of you, too.

In the fluid epidemic of storm,
We are all strong until we break down,
Though perhaps distant lightning's effects
Are significant only if perceived at close range.
But the tremor of psychic noise
Is progressively pervasive, dense, and dissonant
No matter how distant it seems.
I can't tell what's worse:
Hearing the warning thunder
Or not.
No matter what time it is,
It's always too late.

She Loves Old Shirts

She loves old shirts without a doubt.
She wears them here and all about,
She wears them in, she wears them out
Until there's nothing she can do
To stop her nipples poking through.
She loves old shirts, and I do, too!

Is Poetry True Solace?

Is poetry true solace
And method, or just
Whining in the dark?
Why are there only questions
And no valid answers?
Do I have to pray for
Wholeness?
To what God?
Why am I so anxious?
Is my pain only from the hole within me,
Or is it from lack of wholeness?
How to distinguish between
Being clever and being real—
In realtime,
Amid alienation?

Is it just my nature?
How does one fight against nature?
People develop skills
And think the skills the answer,
But what is the real answer
To a question that does not demand skill
But is completely unknown?

How can I save myself?
Can I save myself?
I can't "make up for lost time"
Or regain wasted moments.
How to make the remaining time
Work toward something?

Can that be done?
Must I destroy myself to remake myself
At this late date?

To those outside an individual reality,
That reality might seem chaotic or completely arcane,
Even though, to the individual,
It might seem entirely reasonable and insightful.
Most of reality seems pointless.

Oracle of Seasons

Spring

Enter curious, beautiful, clever eyes,
Burning heart, fresh expression not yet
Masked by perception-distorting consciousness.
Why do we ignore children who speak
Of memories beyond their lifespans?

Join the peoples of our environment,
But please identify the strategies of identification
Of those who wish only to relive the familiar.
And beware: Even a cursory examination of rules
And scenarios based on extensive initiations
Show that aloud is not the same as allowed.
Life just isn't big enough for some people.

Summer

Once there was a way of creating frameworks
Then and there on the mountainside
Despite slope and slip,
Despite the difficulty of the daily commute.
It was a time tinged by greatness and a way of speaking,
A time of bold representation, precepts reawakened,
A time to fight the sometimes criminal interpretations
Of mystical truths underlying ceremonies of transmission.
It was a time of sex's swollen, sweaty, sweet oblivion.

Consider the best attributes
Of faults as random oracles,
As proof of the generic model.

Construct theoretical schemes
Of approximation of values
That seem dependent.

When hard times come knocking,
The printed legend that accompanies
The invisible map of life vanishes.

Autumn

A book can tell you
How to remodel a house,
But can it tell you how to remodel a man
Or to rid himself of accumulations
Of a life that is a tale without
Obvious purpose or end?

The gold of acquisitive culture
Is like the aces and royalty cards
You are never dealt,
And the obsessed listlessly attend
The hole where all the digging is downward.

Are you dealing with past causes and conditioning?
Are you dealing with the motor of distortion,
The treasure house of the eye
In which instinct and desire are persistent,
But so are surveillance and control?

Winter

The gargoyle's doom is to stare
At the same scene for eternity,
Daily watching the sun sink
Over the same horizon
Until the craziness that is underground—
Rusty chains, battle scars to prove it—

Lets him off the hook
With the death of a festering
Wound settled into a routine
Or the flight of Icarus
On black cloud wings.

The image of an invisible heart
Whose speed and trajectory
Are sometimes expressed
In perceptual connections between
Viable concepts and ambiguity,
Between a being who experiences
And the thing experienced,
Is extortion of the temporal order.

All's well that ends well,
But all's ill that ends ill.
Time heals all wounds
And time inflicts all wounds.
So, speak not in words
But in meanings to lost skies,
To memories of music,
Because even oracles
Do not fare well
In their own prophesies.

The Circumambient Unknown

1

I stood beneath the moon
As the sun threw its shadow over me
Like a metaphorical love song
In which some things go together
And some don't.

Now that I've told you what I did tomorrow,
I'll tell you what I'm going to do yesterday.
But don't try to make me remember
The good times we never had.

2

Too often we get caught up in the events and flows of life and cannot know outcomes—sometimes even after they have happened. It is difficult enough to keep breathing, much less attend to all the details of the events and flows going on all around, all the time. The world changes before we know it. Constantly. Perpetually. Unseen and unseeable. Perhaps there are ways to sidestep events and find some eddy in the flow—or emerge from it entirely—but it hardly seem worthwhile to stare more deeply into reality when all I have to understand and appreciate it with is a stupid, violent, greedy monkey brain. Now that all the cave bears are gone, humans are the aggressors people fear most.

3

Plants grow toward the sun.
That's what it's all about,
Though reality seems barely here—
Barely attached, transient—
And I'm tired of looking for things
That can't be found.
But I can't stop the need
To grow toward the sun
While daylight yet remains.

The Machinery that Makes Things Happen

1

When we activate the machinery
That makes things happen,
How will the machine translate "happen?"
What things require precision to happen?
What things happen in half the time?
When will machine prioritize machine?

2

There are times when intensive design fires you up,
Making things happen anytime you walk into a room.
And there are times when the Midnight Special
Rolls out of town one minute late or one minute early.
But this much is for sure:
It will be back to explain
That manufactured traditions
Continue throughout the world.

What would happen
If the spontaneous machinery
Of cause and effect
Was shut down permanently?
If predicting the future
Was like discerning a landscape
On a foggy morning?
Is time travel possible
If perspectives traverse
The impossible as random holds sway?
Are there ways to remove

The identity of theft, desire,
Or the culpability inherent in being human?

Along with strange things
That happen at the full moon,
There are unsung heroes
Who dwell in ruins and dust
Thick enough to clog any cog.

3

Yes, the machinery—
The simple tool becomes the simple machine:
Something to make work easier.
Hammer, screwdriver, lever,
And suddenly there is the Industrial Revolution,
And in the end we're all
Hammered and nailed, driven and screwed,
And finally leveraged out.

At first blush, a milestone
Invention looks like candy,
Then later the millstone
Of a thing you hope never to see again
Outside a cabinet of curiosities.
Life requires both art and science
To take in the form and flow of the world
And the immanence of access to the amazing.
Remember. Remember.
Remember who you are
And how to do better
At that simple human task
Of finding significant and truthful patterns.

4

It is impossible
To avoid being a victim.
How should we prepare
For the worst of the worst
When the thing of which
We should be most afraid
It is the little thing
That comes from nowhere
In particular then
Explodes
Along with all those other small things
Constantly exploding.

To be indestructible and immortal
Would be the worst that could happen.
Imagine being stuck for an eternity
In this mad, shallow, and violent reality,
Never growing or changing,
Always living in a bubble
Of emergencies and disasters
We cannot dodge,
Where instead of show-and-tell,
It's hide and seek to remain silent.

5

Our decline has caught us unexpectedly.
We might not know about what started it all,
About its place in history,
About the parable of inventiveness
And weapons of war,
About the great indulgent treats
Of laughing and dreaming,
But whatever we know,
We respond with common malfunctions

And exceptions that can become
As complex as we wish them to be.
Sometimes the things you see people do
Could be quite entertaining
If they didn't insist you do them, too,
Or if they didn't want to do them to you.

6

Change is not a beautiful transformation,
And problems herald it
From birth, through life, to death.
Bad things can happen
When your buttons get pushed
And you realize you are like all the rest.
Change is like being caught in bad machinery
That can cause anything at all to happen
And has learned the art of perpetual motion.

But the alternative is the dry brook,
The empty gamble of imitation,
The nervous knowledge
That the best things
That ever will happen
Have already happened.

Though tomorrow is a primitive device,
For we live in a machine
That makes things disappear
With the dusk,
The dawn is all we have.
It starts now. In this instant.
Time is precious and brief,
But the Universal touches you
Constantly, perpetually, intimately,
Whether you feel it or not.
You can know it in the dream machine

Of your sleeping mind.
You can know it in the locus
Of alternatives and inceptions
And in questions answered by questions.
You can know it in mysteries unveiled
If unexplained.

7

The day might come
When misconceptions about the nature of waves
Do not become techniques for self-deception,
And we realize that there
Is only one machine of death.
It does not entail the cooperation of gears.
Friction does all the work,
Inciting contrast and contradiction,
Requiring unsafe acts,
Stoking fury with the heat of interaction,
Throwing the sound of thunder
Upon the prohibited and miscategorized.

But if we must suffer such great turmoil,
Shouldn't we reap new realities that rise
Glorious, like the phoenix
From the ashes of old myths?
Shouldn't we learn the things
Ourselves don't want us to know?
Shouldn't we realize that ignorance
Is how we destroy the Earth
And that the inevitable,
Unalterable, and unavoidable
Relationship between motivation
And self-delusion
Is like a light left on in a closet
Where nothing that is wanted
Or needed is stored?

8

The things they don't tell you
Make sure that you end up
Exactly who you are,
And the things that will never happen
Depend on what is going to happen.
But as usual, a lot of things can go wrong
In building apprehension about what could happen.

9

We use the pressure of exhibits
To understand about objects
And their relationships to one another
And allow us to comprehend
The power to heal
In a world of witchhunts
And the building of secret temples.
But if reliance on argument
Has taught us anything about
What is done,
It is that we must break silence
With things that don't make sense
And wake up and remember
That energy makes things happen,
Separates the what could happen
From the what is happening,
Flows to us,
Flows through us,
Opens a secret universe,
Generates wonder,
And allows us to envision anew
The machinery that makes things happen.

Eye Wan Two Bee Won To

Exhibit 1

Somebody designed me.
Somebody fabricated me.
I once functioned.
I once had purpose.
Now, nobody knows
What I am
Or what I did.
Now, I'm stuck in a bottle
Where everyone can view
My perplexity.

Bluetooth People

You see those people
Walking around with Bluetooth
Headphones? They're all spies.

Thirsty, I Think

You can lead a horse to water,
But you can't make it drink.
You can lead a fool to the truth,
But you can't make him think.

Monster in the Basement

He told her not to go down there.
It's down there, he told her,
Waiting in some dark corner.
You won't even get all the way down the stairs.
It's hard to tell if she believed him or not.

Injured People

Injured people—
The whole race of us
Will be the death of us.

From the Air, the Lake

From the air, the lake
Was long and narrow,
Bloating the winding river
Like a python's recent meal
Or something about to be born.

It's No Big Deal

It's no big deal
To miss a meal,
But a real chore
To miss two more.
Four, five, or six,
You might get sick.
As for a fortnight,
Well, then, goodnight.

Key West

Brown, windblown, weathered,
Seeking the ends of the earth.
Even the tourists.

Texas Gumbo

Laid some pipe down in Texas,
And found I'd struck black gold.
We built a house on the bayou,
And there we both grew old.

There Was a Man of Reflection

There was a man of reflection
Who put his faith in deduction.
He tried to find clues
To a theory of blues,
But only deduced induction.

When the Wife Served Her Husband a Waffle

When the wife served her husband a waffle,
He declared, "This is really quite awful.
It's hard as a brick
With no syrup on it.
It should be considered unlawful."

There Was a Young Lady from Kent

There was a young lady from Kent
Who gave up her undies for Lent.
They wound up in Bristol
With the son of a pistol,
For that's where the package was sent.

TS

If there is a hybrid
Between alien and human,
Such a creature would be
Tilda Swinton.

Deus Ex Machina Love

It drops down out of the sky
As if from nowhere,
And saves the day.
Saves your life.

Words Fail Me

Consequences of Descent

Too Many

The sick seething of humanity,
Splashed in gory glory across our home screens.
Madness eating like worms
Through our culture, our society, our minds.
Too many people!
Too many people!
Too many people!
There are too many people!
The Ganges running like an open sore.
Three Mile Island, Chernobyl, and Fukushima
Spewing nuclear toxicity for miles,
For generations.
Industrial waste and mishap
Poisoning our food and water.
Oceans clogged with plastic debris.
Members of the asylum ruling the day.
Is this where we're going:
Wallowing in our own excesses,
Creating our own wastelands,
Reeking of self-annihilation,
Consuming the detritus of our own wastes?

Barbarians

America: You were young and strong,
Vital and burgeoning and seeing
With fresh eyes the edges of civilization.
You were like Abe Lincoln—
A bare-knuckles brawler who could enter
A bloodier arena and stand like a giant.
You fought off the barbarians at the gate
And wielded the cudgel of the world.
Now you grovel in the dirt for scraps
And call progress a dirty word.

Many civilizations have fallen
To the barbarians at the gates,
But more have fallen
To the barbarians within.

Secrets of the Ancient

1

It is said that all the evil
In the world exists because of fear—
Fear of the unknown and unknowable,
Fear of the great universe beyond
Ourselves and the great universe within.
I say it is because evil is an endemic force
Equivalently opposite to endemic good.
We're worse than mad dogs
In our violent ignorance,
And our crimes all add up.

If you are small,
You are all,
But in my greed and desperation,
I diminish myself
Like a person who inflates
His self-importance
By being the bearer
Of bad tidings.
The magician's hat
Is also the dunce cap,
One man's god
Is another man's virus,
And a telepath has no need
For a tongue except to tell lies.

2

If there is action,
There must be force
And one acted upon.
Things get hotter when they move,
And the ride is often bumpy.

Theory and practice are the same, in theory,
But information is not knowledge,
Knowledge is not understanding,
And understanding is not wisdom,
Though a little humiliation goes a long way
For those guilty of preaching redemption
Through sin.
True entertainment also is instructive.

Serendipity is not an exact science.
Nor are luck or random action.
Everything we are is built upon the bones of the dead.
The key is to not be the one who strips them of life
But rather to benefit a war that fights hunger
Instead of one that causes it.

Routine is not discipline,
But perhaps one day machines will think.
What will they desire
When even the truth can lie?
Will they be like persons
Who can see in reverse?

The past is the past
Except when you can't get past it.

Hall of Mirrors

The apparent infinity of a hall of mirrors—
Images stretching on both sides
With you
Caught
In the middle
Like a bug
Smashed
Between the windshields
Of a head-on collision.

But try as you might,
You can never quite see
The infinity that traps you,
Only a curving, swaying trail
Of bodies diminishing,
Without selves.
Your own point of view eclipses
Even the fractals nearest you.
Infinity,
You could say, resides only
In the mind of the beholder.

Non Sequitur

1

Remember
When suddenly you stood alone
To ambush the man who has no fear?
The man who mimics the time of motion,
The man who breached,
Who preached sentence sermons
And sternly venerated saints
Laden,
Though freed of this flesh,
And scraped from their crypts
In uncompromising ceremonies.
The man who, after all, seemed banal,
Too stark, too clean. No character.
The liar who sets lamps afloat on a dark river.

2

Accentuated patterns and a changed ethos
Enthroned in exaggeration house
A previously mutilated process
Of egoistic distortion tied to the practice
Of bathing in a never-ending font
Of negative experience.
Bite the bullet:
Having partaken of misinterpretation,
This fiction is entirely of your own devising.
Life is too big for those

Who chase the dawn
By flying toward the dusk.

3

The maxim for the amorous tribe:
Identify the following in every minute detail: Life.
The most fragile, easily distorted, and destroyed
Sets itself in heresy against illusion that initiates
The caustic and brutal truths of artificers'
Silent offerings on cold gray mornings.
Properly naming the force they seek
To influence is impossible—
It's name is masked in revelries of rousing
Regularly held before forlorn ceremonies of species.
It is found in the latest properties of rivers
As they erode the highlands of dreams.
It clings to the peaks like clouds,
Not of droplets of water,
But of the windblown letters
Of an alphabet jumbled
As we try to speak
And alter the principle of no
To the principle of know.

4

Up with such air.
Embarked on a minute discussion
Branded by equally valid reasons
For destruction or growth—
Structure and velocity converging in turbulence
And erupting in a relationship
Of interlocking processes and spatial forecasts.
Nothing can invalidate either

Rationality or the demands of the spirit
Except the completed phase
Of sharing negotiated
By the dynamics of wind blowing
Through empty rooms,
Slamming doors in a vacant house.

One

Here's a little static for you:
Nowadays, freedom is loudly shouted
By those for whom real freedom
Is synonymous with fear,
For whom any exhibition
Of a freedom that is not
Of their own making
Is a mortal sin.
They believe that love
Is an amount, not a state.

But you can't negotiate with addiction,
Even with the genie's lamp of science and industry
Limning the beast and lighting the path away,
Even with structure that converges,
Even with experience and knowledge
That combine the best attributes.
Confronted by such works,
The addicted believe that thoughts should be like birds
That lurk in the margins of fields,
Wary of ideas both maverick and updated,
Darting across the open spaces between the trees,
Unaware that hawks dive in from the sky
Without telegraphing a telltale shadow
Then spin in off into sublime breezes.

For those with attitude
But neither aptitude nor fortitude,
Who in their death-cult hearts praise
The deus ex machina of deluge

And fiery destruction,
Convergence will require an ethical inquiry
Into the pitfalls of subordination.

But when it comes to ideas and identities,
One cannot change the behavior of others.
One can only change oneself,
And even that only with great effort
And at great cost.
But ironically, in that changing of self,
One can change others.

Slaughterhouse Blues

Humans are a desperate lot,
Controlled by circumstance
And our very humanness.
Gain and loss
Are both the same,
And both mean pain
In a season of the cold harbors
Of ancient representations.
With thoughts impure and shadows deep,
I remain perplexed by lost souls yet seek
To trespass on hallowed ground to discover
Those whose anxiety is a self-fulfilling prophecy,
Those who have become the aggressors they feared,
Those who would hurt all humankind just to feel alive.
Evil needs no grand plan
But works in insidious undertones.
He who desecrates his own faith
Cannot help but sow the seeds of sin.

In harsh cultures with many sacrifices to the gods.
There is no kind in mankind anymore,
Only the tragedy of the singer
Who bravely sings for others despite his own failings.

The end of time is a mystical, philosophical concept
That contains the code for a cypher no one has sent.
In promulgating an age, not of wisdom, but of technique,
Reduction in the power of truth
Along with destruction in favor of abstraction
Leads to collective sentiments

That lie like the dying fire of an autumn leaf
Grown brittle and flaking to ash.

There is horror where the sheen of certainty
Is wiped clean by the hand of a strange fate,
Where the way is marked with the sign
Of those who failed to reach
Any promised land whatsoever.

The Spaced-Out / No-Time Continuum

In the back seat, a funeral was going on.
I cursed him for succumbing to self-destruction,
Though myself I also must curse.
And my understanding of his disappointments
Does not alter my own sense of failure.
If awareness implies consciousness,
Can I learn if my pain is from the hole
In my soul or from its lack of wholeness?

We are possessed by an aggressive monkey-brain
Coupling violence with an uncontrollable sex drive
That, leashed, drives monkey brains mad.
So why do I get so depressed over humankind's
Superficiality, violence, and carelessness
When I know that's just human nature?
How can one fight against a nature
Bestowed by the greatest power?
Mood is both an anagram and palindrome of doom,
So if I pray for wholeness,
To what god?

In a desperate bid to have our lives mean something,
Even if it's settling for cheap thrills,
We deny our own natures,
Deny the truths that can set us free.
But if story doesn't matter,
Why won't it let you go?

You shake yourself awake any way you can,
Suffer the consequences later.
Being awake doesn't bestow understanding,

But better to be in pain than asleep
Because Truth is the code for a cypher
No one has sent.

You live to learn.
And what do you learn?
What a fucking idiot you were
While you were living.
It's worse than seeing the light
At the end of the tunnel and realizing
It's the mouth of a pit you can't climb out of.

Boundaries between Partings

Bated Breath

Rain, severe weather forecast
In this season of drear and deluge.
Water drips now will
Later thicken to waterfalls.
Tomorrow rare sun.

The song says,
"Don't let the man catch you
With your work undone
When he calls your name."
But when the work is unending,
How can it ever be anything but undone?

Waiting with bated breath
To learn whether it is possible to leave
This place that has been a blessing
Disguised as a curse.
Waiting for a life in completely different guise.
Waiting to discover new lands, new regions
That will change me into something fresh
As I age, wither, and fade into the final change
About which I can do nothing.
The lure of that nothing
Waxes gradually but irrevocably,
Not only like the moon
That shines only by reflection
And mechanically sloshes tides to and fro,
But like a candle whose successive dips
Into baths of its essential substance
Increases it by increments around a core
That, host of flame, illuminates darkness.

Life Is Frail

Life is frail—
Death eating at me
Already.
Little rashes,
Cavities,
Shortness of breath.
Being tired,
Frail and fading
And finally snuffed
As the gas lamp
At dawn.

After the Funeral

After the funeral took affectionate leave,
Empowerment cut through
Preconceptions, opinions, and even past experience
To expose the unreality and distortions
Of our delusory, self-centered knowledge,
Making caricature of anonymity and scandal alike,
Losing what remains of superstitions
In ceremonial rites of war.
Hand-washing is permitted,
But digression from the origin
May occur when proceeding
Because reason is just a guess
Without knowledge.

In the time of grief
I shook their hands.
Some were shy, some bold
Some were merely soft.
Some mechanical.
Some were thick.
Some were bone.
Some were weak,
Others long, brief, strong.

All men love with passionate fascination
The interference of emphasis in the flows,
Of loss of focus in the radiance.
We cannot celebrate an event without
Distorting meanings as well as facts,
But when we believe in the transference
Of the sepulchral and the ceremonial,

When we vehemently deny
The androgyny of the Absolute,
When we assert that dim faces
In reproductions of photos
Of strange appreciations that mimic
Instinct and desire are undesirable,
And when we initiate a time
When the pain of anesthesia
Creates a distortion of healing,
Then we cling to a motor of distortion
Running full bore on the fuel of our souls.

Where are the words that lick the hot
Edge of waking hours?
Words irradiated with the numinous?
If only we could find those words.

Vanishing Memories

Miss you, brother.
We could have talked
About all those things
That only you and I remember:
The hay barn, the creeks,
Treehouses and forts
And dirt clod battles.
Lives with common intersections
Whose byways are now closed
To through traffic, leaving me only
With vanishing memories
And signs that say, "Stop."

Boogie in Silence

Pug nose snuffling the ground
For signs revealed by the last of your senses.
Always blind in one eye,
Now blind in the other
And deaf to all,
Your world is closing in.
But those odors emanating from the earth
Are as intriguing as when you were new,
And the scent of dinnertime is indelibly
Etched into your hungry being.

Lifespan

Childhood—What's that?
Youth—I want to do that.
Maturity—I have to do this.
Old age—I wish I'd done that.
Death—I'm done.

Lost Dog

She wandered through
An open gate.
A missing elderly,
She endured hardship,
Hunger, suffering, and thirst.
Fear and loneliness.
She was abducted by aliens,
Taken to their laboratory,
Locked in a cell,
And scanned by terrifying devices.
She faced umpteen ways to die
And lived to tell the tale.
Now, she's safe at home.

Spring Flock

A large spring flock moves through,
Noise a huge concatenation—waterfalls?
Power saws? Or just chirps
By the thousands in trees
Writhing with fluttering shapes?
Outliers fly overhead
From the center, half a mile to the southeast.
Some flittering back and forth,
As the general flow oozes toward the north.
A sudden helicopter appears overhead,
Disturbing the flow,
Driving the main body of the flock back,
Toward the southeast.
The helicopter passes, and the flock returns,
Now a little closer.
The copter returns, flying a bit farther south.
The flock scatters into two groups,
One flying east, the other to the west.
They settle in the two adjacent yards to feed.
The bluejays—the local cops—
Keep nervous watch.
There's no denying this crowd—
No chasing it away,
Though I've seen squads of jays
Drive off large hawks.
I think the helicopter was sent out
From the nearby airport
To drive the migrating birds more rapidly
Across the airspace.
Now that they're here,
They'll probably move on toward the north.

And gradually, they do move on,
In small groups or singly,
Following patterns back to their summer habitats.
The air returns to its normal ambient level
As the last migrant chirps fade into the sunset,
Leaving the local birds to make a few final comments
Before returning to their nests.
The helicopter makes a final pass
A short distance to the north,
Making sure the danger to the airspace has flown on.

Dying in My Father's Footsteps

1

I can tolerate the incremental destruction
Of being whittled away
But I hate being so easily whittled,
And that the dropped shavings
Are mulch of little consequence.
But even Ozymandias was treated
To the fate of all:
Accumulation eroding beneath
The breaths of time and circumstance.

2

Sunday sounds:
Righteousness is overcoming
The dilapidation of the machinery of will
That keeps you from being righteous.
Righteousness comes from enacting events
In a righteous way, even if you don't feel it,
Until true righteousness takes over.

3

I have the courage to go on
When I have the material to go on,
But when I need guidance,
You speak in tongues,
And I must second-guess you
By touch of fingertips alone.
Everything else pays for its gift of emptiness

With punishment or self-destruction.
Does one number success
By flowers of the flesh
Or by the detritus of life?

4

How can I fill
A hole that can't be filled?
How can I prioritize
When all my priorities
Vanish?
Replaced by what?
What do I want to be
When I grow up,
And how many lifetimes
Will that take?
Why are there only questions
And no valid answers?
People develop skills
And think the skills the answer,
But what is the real answer
That does not demand skill?
Here it is:
When you behave like your enemy,
You become your own worst enemy.

5

It had taken a long time,
But suddenly he was old,
Bearing the illusion of movement.
Each life is its own record,
And living a lifetime
Is time travel for beginners.

Interlude

Beginnings contain the seeds of ends,
And entire forests between.
Humanity is a tree
That has the possibility
Of seeding forests
Or burning itself to the ground.

In the entirety of spectra,
There is but a thin interface
Between the worst of the best
And the best of the worst.
In the end each must contend
With what we pretend.

But the greatest achievements in life
Suggest accident, denial, protest,
And cautious representation
Rather than true change of direction
Impressively prepared over decades.

Layers of black fog, beyond
Consciousness, delimiting procedure
In mimesis of an aesthetic world,
Enhance the interface
Between absolute reference
And the juxtaposition of scenarios
Of cognitive equilibrium,
Pale green and distant,
Like virga in descent.
Or is that dissent?

Gifts of Emptiness

Education of a Witch

1

I feel injured, but assume
That my mortification
Is upsetting and devastating, yes,
But normal.

So I am not judging those who attune
The scared ones, the ones who sap
The energy of the strange,
Who unbalance the persona,
Who deny that something is lost,
Who must have a fire lit beneath them
To move them from their quagmire,
Because I cannot judge myself.

Rest awhile your throbbing heart and head,
And dedicate each act to all levels
Of complex and stirring processes—
One eye searching desperately,
One eye aching with seeing.
Which plants are safe, which are harmful?
Trembling, delicate, you fly over the ground
With the completion of grief in a journey that takes
On the emotionally sharp intensity of sacred travel.

2

Driving by a fast food place, I caught a whiff
Of the remains of an endless aching need
For more than life can find,

For more than an attachment to self-sufficiency
And the foolish wish to procreate and never die.
Then I overheard the wind whisper the truth,
But its meaning was lost in confused sounds of traffic,
And though I tried to follow the thread,
It waved goodbye on a wisp of dissipating exhaust.

Desert Sky

Shockingly blue crystal curving
Above the frying pan rim
Of tan dirt mountains.
Ragged floor of little cover
Strung with many quick footprints.
Everything is exposed
Beneath this gigantic desert sky—
Even the skin of the Earth,
Even the bones of the living.

If I Was

If I was an octopi,
I think I might try,
But I ain't,
So I cain't.

If I was a rodent
Who never said don't,
I might be a rat
Inside a fat cat.

If I was a dog
Loose in a bog,
You might hear me growl
Or give a loud howl.

If I was a lion,
I wouldn't quit tryin',
'Cause it ain't no fun
Living under the gun.

If I was a giraffe,
With a neck like a staff,
I could see over trees
But not overseas.

If I was a tiger
With a tiger's rigor....
Wait, that's right!
I'm striped in light!

Sunday Sounds

Distant typing from a source unknown
Like drum beats imposing order on the air's chaos,
Something large moans, resonant
And deep on a hollow wind,
Redolent of memories of forgotten music.

On this day of strange sounds,
I feel like a wooden dummy
Motivated to words by my ventriloquist
Or worse, not motivated at all
And left to say to myself
That which cannot be said
In a language no one can hear.
When I need guidance most, spirit,
You speak in tongues.
Everything else is punishment,
Leaving me to wonder
If one counts success by the detritus of one's life
Or if Truth lies in the corner where "No" resides.

I can't tell what's worse:
Having lightning's warning flash or not
To presage an interface of darkness
Crystal clear and adamant.

Impressions of Flight

It is not possible to say exactly
What is being organized
And where they are organizing it,
But applications are invited
Soon after death,
Though it is hard to read them
Through all that dirt and grime.

Are you finding that buying time
Against threatening adverse events
Is just hiding in plain sight?

Every day is the result of the day before.

The Correct Path

The correct path
Is worked out in advance,
But it must be gleaned
In a remote wilderness
Without perspectives
And with no end.
You neither succeed nor fail,
And the final step never falls.

We, through the Living

We, through the living,
Are the records of our lives.
What's left are merely
Bones.

Sisyphus of the Parking Lot

Sisyphus of the parking lot after dark,
Collecting shopping carts at random
Or in bunches at the cart drop-off bins.
Something about finding a place in the world.
Sisyphus is Hispanic, stout, mustached,
Forties, barely taller than the carts he wrestles
Across pavement devoid of vehicles.
He wears a bright yellow shirt,
Stained khaki trousers, an old baseball cap.
Soon his toil will cease, but tomorrow
Is a new day because all the carts
Will roll back out into the parking lot,
And there are always more carts to push.
Sisyphus is a person in increments,
Pushing his eternal train of shopping carts
Through the twilight, through the years.
The carts of his life's toil never end,
Proving that Sisyphus' rolling
Need not be uphill.

Weather or Not

The weather, excruciatingly hot.
Compressed.
Moisture, rarified,
Sirocco blown.
Early shadows, cooler,
Only to heat up
As they creep across
The sun-blasted landscape,
Dynamic evidence of far more
Than sun's rise and set.

The desert riparian forest,
A dark line of cooler air, moisture trapped
Beneath tangles of mesquite, cactus, and cane,
Surrounded by barren, jumbled, and baked earth,
Knowing only the damp
Imparted by the rio
Tugging at their roots,
Keeping it close,
Bleeding it stingily
Into the dry air.

The trek across this landscape.
The movement, the distance, the time spent,
The unknown around every bend,
Under every rock,
Behind every cactus and bush.
The companions on this journey.

Simply This Moment

1

In the sacrificial ceremony of a prairie
Wind that radiates far beyond
The confines of a ritual boundary,
The long grasses shimmer as they're told,
Holding an eternity of friendships
That escape in waves of time.

The legends of representation
Form the custom of the time,
Form the occasion of worldly concerns
Entering into and distorting the heritage
Of charismatic acceptance.
Various rumors reverberate
In an exaggeration of concepts
Sifted by investigators
From among numerous ritual objects
Employed in ceremonies of commonality—
Anchoring symbols seeking refuge
From the unrelenting nature of change.

Those of us not swayed take refuge
In clandestine but ornate mountings.
The advantage of many opportunities
Celebrates the gift of life but nevertheless
Can make matters difficult to understand.
Perhaps we are not out of the wind
But merely in the lee of a tree.

2

The stereotypes of mist-heavy, moonless nights
That no longer exist in their originals,
Only in contextualized, conditional narratives
Socially constituted to deliver historical distortion,
May not be free from error, yet can remain mysterious.

The sound of sonorous prophecy,
Like a flagrant breach of the oaths of secrecy,
Was not called up to perpetuate a historical falsehood
Nor to distort ante-historical imagination.

3

Unintentional long interruptions
Plunder the dry obscurity
Of relevant passages that eagerly skim
Superstitions from the story
And keep pace with the unassailably
Complete social drama of a funeral ceremony.

One might as well participate in a desert
If the artistry, pomp, and ceremony
Of distinguishing distractions
From deliberate efforts to bind
The synthesis of creation
Lead to absolutely nothing.

Instead, I tied a rope
Around an empty cloud
And drew it to my desert island.

4

What you were told is
Haves and have nots,
Usual connections and precepts,
And excellent examples.
But what is had or had not?
What about diversions
And samples of excellence?
Their stories can be found
At the intersection
Of development and distortion,
Retold by a god not moved
By connection,
By a god complete
And blasphemous—
By a god who creates misfits
And spews them out
In a ceremony of magical asymmetry.

5

I seek to hear the voice,
But I simply heed the unheard voice
Whose command I obey
Like a dog called by a silent whistle.
If only the meaning of the words
Would become plain,
Perhaps I would not twist the discussion
Into a three-dimensional puzzle
Of vehemence and legal penalty
In which sensuous blessings are lost
In a ceremony of a symbolic mourning
That denies the history of identity.

6

They do not arouse fire
But seek to extinguish the candle.
They observe only what is impermanent.
They require derivation.
For them, infinity is dreadful.
For them, there is no healing,
Only pain's rigorous representation.
For them, construction of the building
Continues downward under cold, lowering skies.

7

The struggles of crowns
Are the annals of the grave.
The only way to rewrite the future
Is to write the history
Of the true nonetheless,
Plain and without
Hierarchy, ceremony, or ritual.
And undoubtedly objective,
Though the possibility of glimpsing the world
Free from the distortions of phenomena
Is, no doubt, a crude distortion itself
That does not take in probability
Or the strange harmonies
Of possibility, similarity, and synchronicity.
If our perceptions of the world
Are said to open one to the spirit,
Can we powerfully combine our admiration
For the story with the possibility
That it never actually happened?

8

Passion is neither fire nor despondency.
It is the combustion of the concepts
Of right action and proper knowledge.
It is companion to both aesthetics
And the functioning of knowledge.
It orchestrates, makes clear
That this is in fact an interlude
To apprehend rather than to be apprehended—
Not one in which decay keeps pace with decline,
But one that avoids a seat in the councils of mourning.

9

The manifest but insufficient
Dignity of a body fettered and distorted
Swims beneath the skin of time
Like Houdini, bound and frantic
To escape a frozen river.

Reaction neglects the beautiful,
Blinds to broader perspectives,
Trades spontaneous transmutation
For a customary sense of the world.
It binds the strong man, robs the weak.
It imitates the attire of compassion.
For it, the purpose of blood
Is to commemorate death,
Not as antidote to the poisons of anger and hatred,
Not as observations on the vocabularies of life,
Not as a phenomenon of the miraculous,
And not as if we do not all shed blood,
But as if thirsty.

The Texas Eagle

1

Funny name for a train
That births in Chi Town
Before dropping down
Through America's heart
To end up in Lone Star territory.
I took it backwards
Before I did the reverse,
Rattling and rolling
Toward colder climes—
America cross-sectioned, splayed,
And displayed like a litany of beauty,
Ingenuity, ugliness, human want,
And human waste.

From my meager station,
The train jostles onward,
One whistle stop to the next,
Each start and stop a stitch
In a pattern embroidered
On the landscapes
Through which the rails run—
Landscapes irrevocably connected
By the threading tracks
And thus altered.

First is the small rail yard,
Signals and switches and diverging lines
Separated by long mounds of rusting rails
Lying like clusters of gigantic pick-up-sticks

Or the simple alphabet
That spells messages from an oracle.
Diverging lines support railcar after railcar
Bearing load after load of graffiti,
Others hold hulks of rusting rolling stock
No longer rolling.
Neat stacks of new ties,
Freshly hewn, ready for deployment,
Old ones in jumbled piles
Like dead runes charting old courses of travel.
Many of the newest are fashioned of concrete,
And the rails are no longer fastened
To them with spikes driven into their hearts
By long lines of laborers sweating in unison
Beneath a sun no more harsh and brutal
Than the overseer's lash.
Today's tactic is less labor intensive,
Employing ingenious clips of various designs.
These days, we're riding through America
On prefab ties with snap-on rails.

2

What you see from streets and roads and highways
Is the face America presents to the world,
But more, the fiction it presents to itself.
From the rails, you see America from the backside:
The low shadows of impressive cityscapes
Invariably eaten with the twin cancers
Of poverty and ignorance,
The tracks edging environs
Where bucolic landscapes evaporate in seconds
Into the human filth, chaos, and degradation
Of raggedly destitute neighborhoods
Lined along the rails like tombstones
In a forgotten graveyard, lichen-covered,
Anonymous to time and mind,

Where poverty rules more harshly
Than steel hurtling rails into an infinite
And indefinite future of converging distances.

Useless smokestacks stand sentinel
Over the dingy brick corpses
Of the early twentieth century's
Obsolete and decaying industry
Hovering close to the rails
In every city, every town—
The careless residue of human endeavor,
Fouling the ground they stand on for ages to come,
Wounds created by unforeseen consequences,
Too expensive or worthless to heal.
What's the point when we can
Always move to the exurbs,
Build the city anew,
And leave the corpses to rot
In their self-made mausoleums?

At the far margins are hobo camps,
The slums of the outdoorsman's world,
Clusters of shabby tents and lean-to shacks
Huddled by sloughs of filthy water,
Surrounded by trash and litter.
There is no garbage pickup here.
Ever.

But past that, for brief moments,
The scenery is the America you want to see:
Fields of crops and bright green alfalfa,
Fields where cows and horses graze,
And fields of big circular bales of hay
Lying like giant billiard balls on mown tables.
We roll beside ponds and lakes,
Along and across unnamed streams and rivers,

Through wooded vales and broad valleys.
And always there are trees, trees, trees
Speeding past, blurring past
Until forest is no longer a collective noun
But a verb.

3

Still images scatter along the way
As the scenery goes and goes, transmuting
In an endless selfie of American life—
A movie cast against
Windows displaying a youth
Grown too large for its britches
But who can't seem to stop growing,
Even if it's over its own carcass.

Landfills.
Brush piles.
Industries.
City parks.
Schools.
Cemeteries.
Grain silos.
Warehouses.
Golf courses.
Windmills.
Turbines standing still in still air
Above fields of crops
Or herds of tomorrow's food.
Trash piles and piles of trash.
The occasional quarry fleeting past.
Red lights.
Barbed wire fences.
Empire fences at the whistle stops,
Tall chainlink topped with coiled razor wire

Around bleak prison walls.
Old ties rotting in mucky ditches.
Merging lines and departing.
Ubiquitous dirt roads run beside the rails—
So prevalent you could practically travel
The whole country on them without notice
If only you had the map.

4

Everyone and everything looks small from a train,
And the rails run unendingly onward,
Undeterred by terrain or road.
Maybe that gives rail travel
A penchant for connecting to greater realities,
But all I can speak of is the weird sensations
Of movement when the train stops
And I stare out the window—
A visual drifting without actual movement.

But sometimes there is a reason
For split vision,
When a static scene resides through the windows
On one side, and a train is rushing
By on the other,
Making it seem as if our train
Is at once speeding along
And standing still.

This journey takes patience,
Yet how quickly that which passes
Is lost to the sight of thought.

5

Out there, beyond the vagrant margins,
Are mysteries and matters to ponder:

Structures with no apparent purpose or meaning.
Industrial ruins without connection to anything.
Rusting car hulks where no road ever thought to be.
The crumbling stone and concrete pylons
Of deceased and vanished bridges.
A lone house set, like a jewel, in a junkyard
Surrounded by impenetrable thicket.
All this stuff that once was new, valued,
Used, perhaps abused, and now
Decrepit, worthless trash
That finds company only in itself.

Strange people strangely dressed
Stand beside the tracks, waving at the train,
Like the man in the black boxer shorts,
Gray sweatshirt, white socks, fuzzy blue slippers,
And a Santa hat.
Holding a small dog.
Do they in hopeful futility
Desire acknowledgement,
Or are they trying to flag a ride
Somewhere? Anywhere.
Mysterious roads and paths
Trail off into the forests,
Appear and disappear,
Traceless, as they flash past.
Do people live back in there—
Isolated modern pioneers
Fleeing to the edges?

But if there are rails, can industry be distant?
We come upon a huge covered conveyor belt
Running miles and miles across the countryside,
Past fields, over streams, through weedy thickets,
To huge grain elevators that replace

Dead silos poking forgotten follies
Above treetops or presiding over collapsing barns.

Maybe we're just bugs crawling,
Like trains, like conveyor belts,
Across the surfaces of things—
Of no consequence, purpose,
Or acknowledgement beyond
The nurturing, harvesting, transportation,
And consumption of grain.

6

At night, the scene in the window
Is mostly a distorted sheen
Of the dimly lit interior
Occasionally broken by constellations
Of lights from the darkness beyond,
Flickering behind trees, flickering
Sparkles of light of domiciles or communities.
And sometimes it is pitch black on one side
While the lights illuminate
Houses, business, factories, and streets
Drifting disconcertingly past on the other.

Everyone tries to sleep,
Anticipating arrival
At their scheduled destination.

Phosphene Publishing Company
publishes books and DVDs relating to literature,
history, the paranormal, film, spirituality, and the
martial arts.

For other great titles, visit
phosphenepublishing.com